The Little
NLP
Workbook

A step-by-step guide to achieving personal
and professional success

Jeremy Lazarus

crimson

The Little NLP Workbook: A step-by-step guide to achieving personal and professional success

This first edition published in 2012 by Crimson Publishing Ltd
Westminster House
Kew Road
Richmond
Surrey
TW9 2ND

© Crimson Publishing Ltd, 2012

British Library Cataloguing in Publication Data

A catalogue record for this book is available from the British Library

ISBN 978 1 85458 572 1

Designed by Nicki Averill
Typeset by Mac Style, Beverley, East Yorkshire
Printed and bound in Italy by L.E.G.O. S.p.A., Lavis TN

Contents

About the author

Jeremy Lazarus is a certified NLP Master Trainer as well as a performance coach with over 30 years' business and sport experience. He is a director of The Lazarus Consultancy Ltd, an NLP-based training company specialising in the applications of NLP in business/work, sport and coaching. His clients include blue chip companies, NHS trusts and elite athletes.

Acknowledgements

There are several people I would like to thank.

My parents, for being my parents. Christine Bearpark, Laura Oates and Derian Parsad for giving me feedback and guidance on earlier drafts. Lisa Wake, my friend and colleague, for her love, support and encouragement, and invaluable guidance. The founders and subsequent developers of NLP and the many NLP trainers who have taught me. My students and clients, whose willingness to learn and develop keeps me on my toes. Alison Yates and Beth Bishop at Crimson Publishing, for their patience, advice and encouragement.

Introduction

Welcome to *The Little NLP Workbook*. Whether you are completely new to Neuro Linguistic Programming (NLP) or have some experience, this book is a concise and practical hands-on guide to help you bring NLP concepts and tools into your life.

By the end of this book, you will be even better able to achieve your goals, take your life in the direction you want, harness your inherent strengths and abilities and overcome commonplace challenges such as:

- nervousness at interviews and presentations
- uncertainty about what decision to make
- disagreements with people.

In this book we bring you some key NLP skills and techniques that you can use immediately in your life. We have chosen to focus on techniques that are simple and easy to digest, and therefore have not included some advanced NLP topics, which may require very detailed explanations. (Have a look at *Successful NLP* (Crimson Publishing, 2010) for more in-depth discussions of NLP.)

NLP was initially developed in the mid 1970s by John Grinder and Richard Bandler by finding out how successful people became successful. It has become a respected and widely used approach to achieving better results faster in all areas of life, and there is a growing body of research to evidence its effectiveness. This book is a brief introduction to this large and expanding field. Because NLP is a developing field, there are slight differences in the approach of some NLP schools.

How this book is structured

One key factor why NLP has become so widely used is that it helps people to achieve their goals. To make this book really useful to you, the central theme will be using NLP to set and achieve your goals, as well as how to improve your life.

- **Part 1** starts with an introduction to NLP, helps you to be clear about what you want in your life, and then gives you the right mindset to achieve it.

- **Part 2** gives you the fundamental NLP communication and influencing skills which are relevant in all situations, and which will help you to achieve your goals more easily.

- **Part 3** contains some important NLP techniques that you can use to address the everyday challenges along your journey, increasing the likelihood of your success.

Each chapter ends with a brief summary of the key points so that you are clear what you have covered.

How to get the most from this book

This is very much a 'how to' book. You will be guided step by step through key NLP concepts and processes, followed by exercises to deepen your learning.

I recommend you try to do your best in all the exercises. Most exercises have an estimated duration for your reference. You may want to revisit sections of this book every few months, either to refresh your memory or because your circumstances change as you progress successfully through your life.

As with any profession, NLP has its own terminology. I keep the use of jargon to a minimum, and use 'single quote marks' to denote NLP terminology or everyday words used in an NLP context.

Using NLP ethically: a quick word of caution

NLP coaching techniques are powerful and are to be used only in a way that is beneficial to you and other people involved. This is known in NLP as 'ecology'. For example, if you want to make changes in your career, what could be the impact on your health, relationships, and family?

Please ensure that the consequences of you making changes are totally positive, or that any minor negative consequences are completely outweighed by the positives (for example the time taken to train for a 10km run compared to the satisfaction and benefits of doing it).

Although many of the techniques in NLP are used by qualified NLP professionals to assist others to make changes in their life, *The Little NLP Workbook* is written primarily for you to use in your own life. I strongly suggest that unless you are qualified in NLP, you limit any use of the NLP change techniques to yourself.

Whilst NLP techniques are increasingly being used by medical professionals, therapists and counsellors, they are not a substitute for medical advice, therapy or counselling if that is what someone needs.

And finally ...

I am passionate about teaching and assisting people to achieve everything they want from their life, and then more. I hope that you will use this book to be even more fulfilled in your life. Enjoy!

Part 1
Setting your direction

In Part 1, we start by explaining what NLP is. We then provide you with a framework to enable you to decide on, set and achieve goals that are in keeping with what is important to you and which are truly right for you. Chapter 5 explains the essential beliefs and attitudes that help successful people to achieve their goals, and which you can use to create your success.

What is NLP?

Neuro Linguistic Programming (NLP) is a series of techniques, communication tools, approaches and attitudes that help people to get better results, faster.

The 'Neuro Linguistic' aspect relates to the language of the mind, ie pictures, sounds, feelings, tastes, smells and self-talk. 'Programming' relates to our patterns of thinking and behaving, which could be seen as similar to computer programs. Examples of such patterns are:

- feeling nervous (or confident) before an interview
- getting annoyed (or laughing) when our child drops food on the floor.

NLP helps you to set goals that are right for you, and to overcome challenges in the way, so that you are far more likely to achieve your goal.

The benefits of NLP

NLP has three main benefits.

1. **Improve communication:** both to influence people more effectively and to change the way we communicate to ourself.

2. **Change your thinking, behaviours and beliefs:** to stop doing things that prevent you achieving what you want and start doing more of the things that will help you to be, do or have what you want.

3. **'Replicate excellence':** if you (or someone else) can do something excellently, NLP can be used to replicate (or 'model') the relevant excellent behaviour(s) and attitudes.

Some of the main uses of NLP

As NLP helps to improve performance, it can be used in virtually every area of life.

Business/work

- Sales
- Advertising and marketing
- Managing people
- Building customer relations and/or supplier relations
- Negotiation
- Conflict/dispute resolution
- Team building
- Leadership
- Presentations
- Recruitment
- Interviews
- Creative problem solving
- Decision making

Coaching

- Helping clients achieve goals
- Increasing overall fulfilment
- Feeling more confident
- Overcoming personal barriers to success

Education

- Learning
- Teaching

Health

There are many health benefits of NLP. Some medical professionals have used NLP, for example, for pain management and weight loss.

Sport and performing arts

- Improving focus
- Overcoming bad performances
- Feeling confident and/or overcoming nerves
- Mental rehearsal/visualisation

Relationships

- Finding a suitable partner
- Improving communications within families

Summary

- NLP is predominantly about achieving better results, faster – how to have more of what you want and less of what you don't want.

- NLP has three main benefits: improving communication, changing thinking, behaviours and beliefs, and replicating (modelling) excellence.

- NLP can be used in all areas of life.

Taking stock

Before you start setting and achieving your goals, it is useful to do the exercise over the page (known as the Wheel of Life) to take stock of where you are currently in your life. This will help you to decide in which areas you may want to use NLP tools to improve your life.

Exercise 2.1
How balanced is your wheel?
(10–15 minutes)

1. List the areas

List what you think are the key areas of your life. Typically there are between six and 10, for example work/career/business/job, finances, health and fitness, partner/intimate relationship, family, friends/social life, personal development, spiritual development, and hobbies.

1 ....

2 ....

3 ....

4 ....

5 ....

6 ....

7 ....

8 ....

9 ....

10 ....

2. Create the wheel

Divide the blank circle on p.20 into the number of segments you have just listed, so that it looks like a wheel. Assign each of the areas a segment to create your Wheel of Life. The order is not important.

3. Allocate scores

Allocate a score representing your current (honest) level of satisfaction for each area, where 10 means that you are absolutely delighted with it and 0 means 'it's the pits'. (NB. It is your opinion that counts, not other people's. For example, if you are not currently in a relationship, and you are happy with that, score it accordingly even if your friends and family are nagging you to find a partner.)

Denote the score with a cross in the relevant segment; so for 10 your dot is on the circumference, and for 1 your dot is close to the centre of the circle.

An example covering steps two and three is shown on the opposite page.

An example wheel

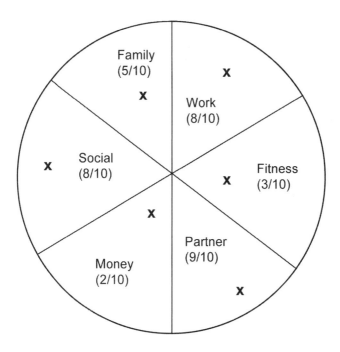

Your wheel

4. Assess

Join up the crosses. How does your wheel look? Imagine going on a journey in a car with wheels this shape and size. A fairly round and large wheel suggests your life is in balance, and that you will have a comfortable, speedy journey. If your wheel is small and round, or jagged (some high and low scores), it suggests a slow or bumpy ride.

Whilst some areas will be more important to you than others, generally life is better if all scores are high. In my experience, the four key areas for almost everyone are health, work/career, relationship and money.

5. Progress

Revisit Exercise 2.1 every few months, with new versions of the circle, noticing your progress as you incorporate the ideas in this book.

Exercise 2.2

Things to change

(10–15 minutes)

Using your scores from Exercise 2.1 and also from the main uses of NLP from Chapter 1 (pp.11–13), list the things in your life that you would like to change, for example improving your level of fitness or changing departments at work.

I suggest you initially work towards making all areas an acceptable score to you, for example at least a 6, and then aim to increase each score. Use this book to assist you in making these changes. If your scores are mainly 9 and 10, what would take the scores to even beyond that?

Areas I would like to work on:

....

....

....

....

....

....

....

....

....

....

Summary

- Use your Wheel of Life to assess how your life is shaping up, and to identify the areas you want to work on in this book.

- Review it regularly, perhaps every year or whenever there is a significant change in your life.

- Once you have identified some areas you would like to change, you can use these to form the basis for your goals.

3 Setting and achieving your goals

An essential step towards having the life you want is to set the right goals for you, and then to take action towards achieving them. In this chapter you will learn the NLP approach to setting goals, which will make you much more likely to achieve them.

The benefits of effective goal setting

- It helps you to take control and to not let others or circumstances direct your life.
- It provides you with direction to focus your energies and efforts.
- It minimises the likelihood of wasting time and energy going for a goal that isn't right for you.
- It helps make sure you are creating the kind of life you want because you will achieve more.

Overview of goal setting

In NLP, there is a concept called 'well-formed' goals. A well-formed goal is formulated in such a way that it gives you the best chance of achieving it. The goal-setting process has four key stages.

1. Decide broadly on the goal.

2. Ask goal-setting questions to help you refine the goal and make it well formed.

3. Use a checklist to ensure that the goal is well formed.

4. After setting the goal, take action to achieve it!

We'll look at these key stages in more detail over the next few pages.

1. Decide broadly

Which area of life do you want to address? What are your initial ideas about which goal to set? For example, if you are unfit, your initial goal may be 'to become fitter'. Refer back to Exercise 2.2 (p.22) to help you with your answer to this.

2. Ask and refine

Once you have a broad idea, ask yourself the following questions to refine and clarify the goal.

1. **What specifically do you want?** State it in the positive, with no negations or comparisons.

2. **Where are you now?** This is in relation to achieving the goal.

3. **What will you be seeing, hearing, feeling, saying to yourself, and even smelling and tasting when you have it?** State it in the present tense, or as if it has already happened.

4. **How will you know undeniably when you have achieved it?**

5. **What will this outcome get for you or allow you to do?** What doors will it open; what's the goal beyond the goal?

6. **Can you initiate/maintain the achievement/progress yourself?** Even if you need input from other people, can you ask for it and make it happen?

7. **Where, when, how and with whom do you want to achieve it?**

8. **What resources do you need?** What do you have now, and what do you need to get your outcome? Have you ever had or done this before? Do you know anyone who has? How did you or they do it?

9. **For what purpose do you want this?** What will you gain or lose if you have it? What will happen if you get it? What will happen if you don't get it? What won't happen if you get it? What won't happen if you don't get it? What is the impact on other people? Will the impact mean that they will try to prevent you?

The purpose of these questions is to help you to be really clear about what you want, and the consequences of getting it, and ensuring that the goal is truly right for you. One of my clients saved £200,000 just by asking herself these questions; she realised spending £300,000 on a business venture would not get her any more benefits than spending £100,000.

Question 9 is a particularly important question. When setting goals, it is essential to consider whether the goal fits with the following.

1. Your own sense of 'purpose' and the impact on others; for example being a role model to your children (by running a marathon), helping the local community (by raising £1,000 via a raffle) or helping impoverished children (by donating a percentage of your company's profit target when it is reached).

2. Your own sense of self (identity); for example are you the sort of person who rises to the challenge of running a marathon/organising a raffle/hitting a stretching profit target?

3. What is important to you in your life or in the particular area of life that the goal relates to (career, relationships, etc). This is known as 'values', and is covered more fully in Chapter 4.

4. Your beliefs about whether you can achieve it. Beliefs are covered further in Chapters 5, 6 and 12.

When my clients and students set well-formed goals that are absolutely in alignment with these four points, they achieve the goals far more easily, feel energised in pursuit of the goal and are more willing to address challenges that may appear. You may have experienced this for yourself, or you may know people who are totally focused on their goal and emit a sense of 'aliveness' and vitality as a result. Conversely, I had an extremely talented client who was doing well yet under-achieving in her law career; she had the skills to be a great lawyer, but her heart was not in it. She was in law because she wanted to please her family; her own desire was to communicate with people through a career in music. When she set a music-related goal, she achieved more in six months than she had in five years as a lawyer.

So when you look at your goal, do you feel really energised and excited at the prospect of achieving it? If the answer is 'yes', then move on to the next stage. If not, either revisit the goal or recognise that achieving it may not be as easy and as much fun as you might originally have thought.

Very occasionally, setting a goal can cause the person to feel internally conflicted or significantly upset, for example if they are setting a goal to please someone else (like the lawyer). In such situations, it may be useful to seek coaching from an NLP professional.

3. Checklist questions

Next, use the following checklist to ensure the goal is well formed.

- Is it stated in positive terms?

- Can I start and maintain the progress?

- Do I know what I'll be seeing, hearing, feeling, etc, when I have achieved it, and is there a specific date?

- Is it truly right for me and others in my life?

- Is there more than one way to achieve this?

- Do I know the first step?

- Will more doors and possibilities open for me when I've achieved the goal?

- Will the positives of the current situation remain?

- Is the goal achievable and realistic for me?

If the answer to any question is 'no', revisit the process and possibly revise your goal.

An additional question is: 'Will achieving the goal help me to have more of what's important to me?' This is covered in Chapter 4.

4. Take action

Now that you have set a well-formed goal, decide on an appropriate first step, however small, and then take action as soon as possible. For example, book a session with a fitness trainer or a financial adviser today. You do not need to know every step of the way to your final goal, because once you have taken the first step, the momentum has started. Keep taking action.

It may be useful to consider the following factors when taking action (let's use fitness and financial goals to illustrate).

- What additional skills or abilities would help you to achieve your goal? For example, improved swimming technique, or more knowledge of the financial world. Who could teach you or provide these skills? What existing skills do you have that you could use?

- What behaviours do you have that are not useful? For example, eating a little too much or reading the gossip section of the newspaper rather than the money section. What behaviours would be more useful instead?

- What aspects of your environment or locality help or hinder? For example, do you dislike and avoid your local gym while you would be more willing to use the gym close to work? Are your financial statements easy to access or hidden in one of 20 piles of papers?

Examples of well-formed goals

Here are some examples of well-formed goals that some of my previous clients have set.

- It is 30 June 2011 and I have bought a semi-detached house with four bedrooms, two reception rooms and a 20-metre garden. The house is five minutes' walk from Guildford station. I feel very happy living here.

- It is 30 September 2011 and I have £10,000 in my savings account.

- It is 31 December 2011 and I have weighed 60kg for the past three months. I feel fit, strong, healthy and energised. (Note how this is different from simply 'to become fitter' as per 'Decide broadly' on p.28.)

Exercise 3.1
Goal setting
(20–25 minutes per goal)

1. Decide on a goal.

2. Ask yourself the questions in stage 2. Refine your goal if necessary.

3. Ask yourself the checklist questions in stage 3.

4. Take action.

Goal A

Well-formed goal: ....

....

....

....

....

....

Action – first step: ....

....

....

Deadline for first step: ....

Goal B

Well-formed goal: ....

....

....

....

....

....

Action – first step: ....

....

....

Deadline for first step: ....

Goal C

Well-formed goal: ....

....

....

....

....

....

Action – first step: ....

....

....

Deadline for first step: ....

Some tips on goal setting

- Separate the setting of the goal from how to achieve it. Having a well-formed goal is the first key step.

- Once you have your well-formed goal, focus your attention on it.

- Keep taking action.

- Ask for help and guidance where appropriate from people you believe would be able to help you.

- Often, it is better to set a stretching goal (eg £10,000) and almost get there (only £9,500) than to set too modest a goal (eg £1,000) and achieve it easily. It may be more challenging, but you will achieve more by doing so.

- Celebrate your successes.

Visualising your success

One additional step beyond standard NLP goal setting is visualisation, which is practised by many successful people including champion athletes. Having set your well-formed goal, find a quiet spot and visualise your success. See a picture of yourself achieving or having already achieved your goal (on an imaginary television or cinema screen); hear the sounds and feel the feelings that are present in the situation. Then imagine that the moment of achieving your goal is happening right now, you are seeing it through your own eyes, also with the sounds and feelings. Adjust your mental picture (perhaps make it even brighter, bigger, closer to you and in clearer focus), and the sounds (volume, pitch, tempo) so that it feels absolutely perfect for you. Feel how grateful you are having achieved your goal knowing that by achieving the goal, even more becomes possible for you afterwards.

Summary

- Setting goals is essential to success and achievement.

- Use the four step process whenever you set goals.

- The important thing is to set a well-formed goal. How you achieve it can be addressed afterwards.

- Set challenging goals to achieve more.

- Visualise your success.

4 Identifying your values

Having set well-formed goals that are right for you, let's take a closer look at 'values'. As briefly mentioned in Chapter 3, values are those things which are important to us in any particular context. They link to our motivation because most people are motivated to have the things that are important to them.

Examples of values could be: in our career – challenge and variety; in relationships – trust and love; in our health and fitness – strength and stamina. We also have values in more everyday aspects of our lives, like which restaurant to go to (eg service and food quality). Values tend to be somewhat abstract or intangible; for example, challenge means something different to different people.

Why are values so useful?

A knowledge of values can help you:

- set goals and be more motivated to achieve them

- better understand what drives you

- make better choices (eg careers, partners, holidays)

- improve your level of satisfaction with situations (eg job, relationship).

Identifying values

You can identify your values by asking a few simple questions. You can do this for all the areas in your Wheel of Life (p.20), and for any purchase or decision, for example which shoes to buy, where to live or which school to send your children to. To illustrate, let's choose the context of 'career'.

Step 1: Ask yourself, 'What's important to me in my career?', 'What do I want from my career?', 'What do I look for in a career?' (Refer back to the second paragraph of this chapter for examples of values.)

- List your values.

- When you have your list, ask yourself, 'What else is important to me in my career?' Add any new thoughts.

Depending on the context, there are typically between five and 10 values.

Step 2: Look at the list. Ask yourself, 'If I had all of these values in a career, would I want it or is anything missing?' If something is missing, add it to the list.

Step 3: Rank the list in order of importance. Do this either:

- numerically, putting a '1' for the most important, a '2' for the next most important, etc; or

- using 'A' for the essential values, 'B' for the important but not essential values, and 'C' for the 'icing on the cake' values.

Choose whichever method is most useful. If you are doing this for greater insight, use the numerical ranking. If you are using it to make a decision, use the A/B/C because it is easier to do and if certain values are absolutely essential to you the numerical ranking probably doesn't matter.

Step 4: As a final check, look at the top four or five values, or the 'A's. Would you want a career with these? If the answer is not a resounding 'yes', review your list and the ranking.

Exercise 4.1

Identifying values

(10 minutes per context)

Identify and rank your own values in different contexts in your life, particularly those contexts where you have set a goal or where your Wheel of Life score is low (p.20).

Context: ....

Value	Rank
....	....
....	....
....	....
....	....
....	....
....	....
....	....
....	....
....	....
....	....

Context: ....

Value	Rank
....	....
....	....
....	....
....	....
....	....
....	....
....	....
....	....
....	....
....	....

Context: ....

Value	Rank
....	....
....	....
....	....
....	....
....	....
....	....
....	....
....	....
....	....
....	....

Context: ....

Value	Rank
....	....
....	....
....	....
....	....
....	....
....	....
....	....
....	....
....	....
....	....

Using values to achieve goals

To increase the likelihood of achieving the goals you set in Chapter 3, ensure that they align with your top three or four values (or all the 'A's); in other words, that achieving the goal means you'll have more of what's important to you. If necessary, revisit the goal(s) you set in Chapter 3 in the light of your learnings from this chapter.

Making choices using values

Once you know your values, you can make choices accordingly. Sticking with your career, let's imagine that your values are those listed in the table opposite and that you have two possible career options (D and E). Indicate in each box the extent to which each value will be met, using scores out of 10 (where 10 means it will be fully met, 0 means not met at all).

Rank	Value	Option	
		D	**E**
A	Challenge	8	2
A	Variety	8	5
A	Learning	5	6
B	Good people	3	9
B	Good salary	8	8
C	International travel	3	5
C	Job security	2	6

Choose the option that gives you more of what is important to you and that feels right.

Exercise 4.2
Making choices
(20–25 minutes, including Exercise 4.1)

If you have an important choice to make in your life, elicit and rank
the values in that area (in Exercise 4.1) and then assess the extent
that your values will be met by each option.

Your options (eg different career options)

A: ....

B: ....

C: ....

Context:				
		Option		
Rank	**Value**	**A**	**B**	**C**

Using values to improve situations

If you want to improve your career satisfaction, identify and rank your career values and then score out of 10 the extent to which each value is currently being satisfied or met. Ask yourself the following.

- What would improve the situation?

- What could I ask for or do to improve the scores?

You can either ask these questions in relation to each individual value, or to the scores overall.

Exercise 4.3
Improving a situation
(15-20 minutes)

Pick an area of your life that you would like to improve. List in the table opposite your values (in order of importance) and your current level of satisfaction (score out of 10).

Context:	
Value	**Relevant actions/requests**

Summary

- Values are what are important to you in any situation.

- Values provide motivation. If your goals and choices fit with your values, you are far more likely to achieve your goals and be happy with your choices.

- You can use the knowledge of your values to improve situations such as your career and relationships.

5 The mindset for success

The developers of NLP found that highly successful people tend to have a specific set of positive beliefs. This chapter covers how to have this mindset to help you to achieve your goals.

The principles for success

Here are six principles for success used in NLP.

1. **Set a desired goal or outcome** before starting any activity or task. Even if it is not a full well-formed goal (Chapter 3), at least know what you want before going to the gym or starting a meeting.

2. **Use your eyes, ears and feelings** (known as using 'sensory acuity') to gather feedback and see whether you are on track to achieve your goal.

3. **Be flexible.** If what you are doing is not working, take a different approach.

4. **Build and maintain rapport**, ie good relationships with people. Rarely can we succeed without the assistance of others. ('Rapport' is covered in Chapter 7.)

5. **Have a positive mental attitude and body language.** A key aspect of NLP relates to thinking and acting positively.

6. **Take action.** This was covered in goal setting and achieving (p.33).

The mindset for success

In NLP, depending on which school you follow, there are around 15 to 20 underpinning beliefs that help NLP professionals in their work. Let's look at five that will be extremely useful in your life. Whilst these are beliefs and not truths, if you behave as though these positive beliefs are valid, and therefore act upon them, they will help you to improve your results.

1. **There is no 'failure', only 'feedback'.** If you don't succeed at a task, taking it as 'feedback' will help you to learn and feel as though you're making progress. If you take it as 'failure', you may feel negative (some people even give up).

2. **Be flexible.** The more flexible you can be, the more likely you are to succeed. Having 1,001 ways to respond is usually better than having only one way. See point 3 of 'the principles for success'.

3 **People have untapped potential.** All of us have inner resources (such as determination, ability to learn, motivation). In Chapter 9 you will learn how to access and channel such resources.

4. **Respect the opinions and individuality of others**, just as you would want them to do with you. You are more likely to influence and build rapport if you do this.

5. **If someone else in a similar situation can do something, then so can you.** Learn from successful people, notice what they do and take on board what you think will help you.

Cause and effect

The mindset for success can be summed up using the concept of 'cause and effect'. For every effect there is an underlying cause. Similarly, people can be either 'at effect' or 'at cause'.

- **At effect** means that we believe that the causes for our situation and problems lie outside us (eg the government, our teachers).

- **At cause** means that we know that, at the very least, we can choose how we respond to negative situations, and in the longer term we can change our mindset and therefore change negative situations or circumstances around us.

People who are at effect tend to:

- blame others
- make excuses
- have lots of good reasons and justifications for not succeeding
- get stuck in a rut
- be miserable.

People who are at cause tend to:

- get results
- succeed
- have a 'can do' attitude
- take total responsibility for their life, and their results
- overcome challenges
- be happier.

NLP aims to move people to being at cause.

Exercise 5.1

How at cause are you?

(3 minutes)

Using the scale of 0–100%, where 100% means you are totally at cause, complete the table opposite. Refer to the bullet points on the previous page to help you decide on your score. Look back at your Wheel of Life (p.20) if you would like to add additional areas to those shown.

Area of life	Score
Life generally	
Work/career/job	
Health and fitness	
Relationships	
Money	

What have you learnt from this exercise? Were you surprised by your scores? What are the areas you would like to address to become more at cause?

Exercise 5.2
Applying this in your life
(15 minutes)

Pick an aspect of your life, for example work.

- Think of two situations that went well and two that did not go well.

- For the successful situations, which of the 'principles for success' and 'mindset for success' factors shown in the table over the page were you (perhaps unknowingly) using (mark with a ✓ in columns A and B)? For example, in that situation did you use rapport?

- In the less successful situations, put a * in columns C or D to denote which of these areas were missing or would have been useful had you known about them.

- In the final row, note the extent to which you were at cause overall in those situations.

Success factor	Well	Well	Not well	Not well
	A	B	C	D
Outcome				
Gather feedback				
Flexibility				
Rapport				
Positive mind and body				
Take action				
No failure, only feedback				
Recognise my potential				
Respect others				
Learning from others				
At Cause (%)				

All of my students and clients say that when they operate from these principles they are more successful, and in situations that don't go well one or more of these principles are not being used. You will probably find this too. I strongly suggest that you use these success factors in future situations to assist you to achieve your goals.

Summary

- Whether they realise it or not, successful people operate from the mindset for success and the principles for success. Use them!

- Be 100% at cause in your life. You'll be more successful and fulfilled.

Part 2
Communication

Part 2 provides you with essential communication skills that are useful in virtually all situations. This knowledge will help you to understand yourself and others more, to be better able to communicate with them and make you more likely to achieve your goals.

Communication
and interpretation

Why is it that we can say the same thing to different people and get completely different responses? In this chapter you will understand how people interpret information, which will help you to communicate more effectively and be more likely to achieve your goals.

The NLP Communication Model

The diagram opposite represents a summary of how people process information. Whenever we perceive an external 'event', we process (filter) it in our mind. Depending on how we filter the event, we will have an internal representation (a mental image, thought or idea about it). This internal representation impacts on our state (how we feel; covered in more detail in Chapter 9), which in turn will be reflected in our physiology (our body language, how we are standing and breathing). All of this influences our behaviours, which ultimately influences our results.

Let's use an example of a group of friends in a restaurant to explain the Communication Model.

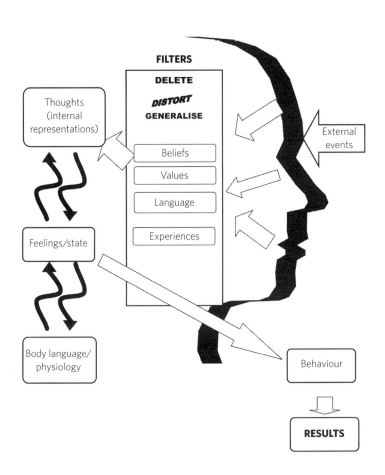

The three overall filters

We initially delete, distort and generalise information. Deletion is where we do not consciously notice what happens because we are limited to how much we can pay attention to at any one time. In the restaurant, one of the friends may not consciously notice (ie they delete) the decor in the restaurant, whereas others may notice it. (Deleting is different from ignoring, which is a conscious decision, for example ignoring that it's your turn to leave a tip!)

Distortion is where we interpret an 'event' as meaning something when it may not mean that or could have other interpretations. For example, if the waiter serves someone last and they think it's because he or she doesn't like them, that's almost certainly a distortion.

Generalisation is where we take a few experiences or bits of information and generalise them to mean that 'things' are *always* like that, or that *everyone* (or *no one*) does that. If the restaurant has sold out of someone's favourite dish, they might say, 'that *always* happens to me', or 'this restaurant *never* has what I want', which is probably an exaggeration.

Exercise 6.1

The Communication Model in action for you

(10–15 minutes)

Think of at least three situations which did not go as well as you had hoped or planned. With the benefit of hindsight, what did you delete/not notice, distort/misinterpret and/or generalise/assume based on past experiences, which contributed to the less-than-ideal outcome. Examples are provided for your guidance.

Deletions

'Meeting': How often my colleague looked at her watch

....

....

....

....

Distortions

'Client lunch': I assumed her looking out of the window meant she was bored

....

....

....

....

Generalisations

'Shop complaint': I assumed all shop people bend the truth

....

....

....

....

Exercise 6.2
The Communication Model in action for others

(10–15 minutes)

This is similar to Exercise 6.1 (with different or the same situations), except that here you should think about what the other person(s) involved deleted, distorted and/or generalised that contributed to the less-than-ideal outcome.

Deletions

....

....

....

....

Distortions

....

....

....

....

Generalisations

....

....

....

....

Key learnings and actions

Other filters

There are some filters which influence what we delete, distort and generalise.

Beliefs

Beliefs are our current thinking about a topic; often, we get tunnel vision about our beliefs and call them 'the truth'. If the waiter takes orders from female customers first, one lady in the group may be happy because she believes in 'ladies first', whereas another lady may be a little offended because she believes in 'equality'.

In addition, beliefs can be either empowering (eg 'I can learn to swim easily') or limiting ('I find it hard to learn new things'). We covered empowering beliefs in Chapter 5. Limiting beliefs are dealt with in Chapter 12.

Values

In the restaurant, people may not notice the decor because decor is not important to them, yet they may notice the ratio of waiters to customers if they are interested in the restaurant's profitability. We covered values in Chapter 4.

Language

The words we use influence the way we and/or others perceive a situation. Compare these two statements made in the restaurant.

- 'You can't dance.'
- 'You haven't yet learned how to dance as well as you would like', or even, 'You can't dance yet.'

The first statement probably limits possibilities, and could cause someone to feel negative, whereas the second statements leave the 'door of possibility' open. The situation could be exactly the same, and yet the way it is phrased will influence the listener. In NLP, language is a huge topic, and we touch on it in Chapter 8.

Using the Communication Model to your advantage

Simply being aware of the Communication Model can help you alter your results. For example, if you know that politeness is a value of one of your customers you can alter your behaviour accordingly.

Also, because states, internal representations and physiology are interrelated, you can alter any one of them to impact the others. We will cover how to do some of this in Part 3. You have probably already experienced how changing your physiology, for example doing exercise, dancing or standing more upright, impacts on how you feel and think.

Some tips on communication

Sometimes it is important that people remember what you have said (ie they do not delete) and/or that they interpret it correctly (ie they do not distort), and/or they listen with an open mind (ie they do not generalise). Examples of situations could be giving safety-based information to your children, feedback to a colleague or instructions to your decorator.

Here are some tips when communicating important messages.

- Repeat or emphasise important points.

- Communicate the message in more than one way (see Chapter 8 for additional examples).

- Give examples.

- Ask people what they are going to do (eg if you have given important instructions) so that you can check whether they have understood.

Summary

- Everyone you meet interprets events in their own unique way.

- We all delete, distort and generalise information based on our beliefs, values, the language we use and our experiences.

- Altering your physiology can change how you feel and think.

- You can alter your communication to influence other people, based on what you now know about the Communication Model.

7 Building rapport

In most situations it is essential to be able to build a spirit of trust and co-operation with other people, so that they are more likely to support you (or at least not hinder you) in the achievement of your goals. This is called 'rapport', and we referred to it in the principles for success (Chapter 5).

Exercise 7.1
When to build rapport
(1 minute)

The table opposite lists some situations when it would be useful to build and/or maintain rapport. Add other situations that are relevant to you and your goals.

Situations where I need to build or maintain rapport

Interviews	Presentations
Meetings at work	Meeting (new) friends
Appraisals	
Selling	
With customers/clients	
Meeting suppliers	
During disagreements	
Going on a date	
Preventing disagreements	
Negotiations	
Coaching	

Some key background principles

1. Up to 90% of communication is non-verbal (voice tonality and body language). You can probably remember specific situations when you knew how someone felt simply by the tone of their voice or their body language.

2. During a typical conversation, we are normally consciously aware of the words someone is saying, and not so consciously aware of the voice tonality or the body language.

3. Generally we feel most comfortable with people who are like us to some degree.

Therefore, if we can non-verbally demonstrate that we are like someone, they will probably feel comfortable with us. This is the basis for rapport building. Almost all of us naturally build rapport with people who we know and like. This chapter is about how to build rapport initially, and how to maintain it in situations where it would be mutually beneficial.

How to build rapport

We can build rapport by 'matching' or 'mirroring' someone's body language and/or voice tonality. Matching and mirroring are similar to each other; the difference being that when you are facing someone who, for example, is raising their right hand, you would be matching them if you raise your right hand, and mirroring them if you raise your left hand.

Here are some of the non-verbal aspects you can match or mirror in a conversation:

Body language

Type	Examples/comments
Gestures	Hand waving, pointing
Posture	Leaning forward or back, legs crossed/uncrossed, hand on hip
Breathing	Adjust your breathing speed (fast/slow) to match the other person

Voice tonality

Type	Examples/comments
Volume	Some people speak loudly, others quietly. Adjust your volume towards where they are.
Speed	Some people speak quickly, others slowly. Adjust your speed towards where they are.

One of the indications of having built rapport with someone is that when you move or make a gesture, or change your voice speed or volume, they follow you.

Common sense is needed

Please note that building rapport is not about manipulating someone or matching/mirroring everything they do; it is about being subtle and using common sense. Here are some tips.

■ During a conversation, only match/mirror someone's gestures when it is your turn to speak (postures can be matched/mirrored regardless of who is speaking).

- Pick only one or two aspects of body language or voice tonality to match, rather than several, otherwise you risk not being able to pay attention to what the person is saying (a sure way to break rapport!).

- A little goes a long way. You do not need to match everything they do, merely some of it. If someone uses big gestures, perhaps with both hands, you could use smaller gestures or use only one hand.

- Do not match/mirror every movement the person does – it will become too obvious and you risk breaking rapport.

The next time you are in a café, bar or restaurant, notice how many people are naturally matching/mirroring the people they are with.

Exercise 7.2
Rapport checklist for important situations

When in a situation where it is important to build rapport (see Exercise 7.1), pick one or two aspects from the list below to match/ mirror, until it becomes automatic for you. When on the phone, match volume and/or speed. Remember the 'common sense' points made earlier.

- Arms

- Legs

- Posture

- Gestures

- Breathing rate

- Voice speed

- Voice volume.

Chapter 8 covers ways of using words to enhance rapport.

Summary

■ You can build and maintain rapport to enhance your relationships (personal and professional) by matching/mirroring physiology and/or voice tonality.

■ You automatically do this with people you know well.

■ Use common sense when matching/mirroring.

8 Speaking everyone's language

This chapter looks at how we all connect with and make sense of situations, and how this impacts our thoughts and responses. You will be able to use this information to communicate more effectively with people, which will improve your chances of success.

Our senses

We gather and process information using our five senses: seeing (visual), hearing (auditory), feeling (kinaesthetic), smelling (olfactory) and tasting (gustatory). These are known as 'representational (rep) systems'. There is a sixth rep system, known as auditory digital, which refers to our 'self-talk' and logical processing/analysis of the information gathered through our five main senses.

Although we all use all of our five main senses plus auditory digital to process information, most people develop a personal preference for one or two, usually from visual, auditory, kinaesthetic and auditory digital.

Why this knowledge is important

If you develop your flexibility to give information according to the way others prefer to receive it (for example having a conversation with, rather than showing diagrams to, someone who prefers auditory) they will be more receptive to your messages. This can make you better at, for example:

- formal presentations

- interviews

- teaching

- meetings

- selling

- general interpersonal relationships.

We will now cover how to identify the sensory preferences of others and present information accordingly. Also, if you know your own preference(s), you could:

- request, if appropriate, other people to present information in the way you prefer

- practise and improve your ability to use your least-preferred sense(s) for when you communicate with people having that preference.

How rep system preferences are expressed in words

If, for example, someone is thinking in pictures, they will usually use picture words and phrases like 'see', 'look', 'focus in' and 'point of view'. Similarly if someone is thinking in sounds, feelings and 'self-talk', they will usually use words that relate to these (see opposite for some examples). In NLP, these sensory-linked words are known as 'predicates'. If you want to build rapport and influence someone, it is important to match the type of sensory language they are using; if someone is using auditory predicates, use auditory predicates in response.

Here are some examples of predicates:

VISUAL
See
Look
View
Appear
Show
Illuminate
Clear

AUDITORY
Hear
Listen
Sound
Tune in/out
Quiet
Explain
Ask

KINAESTHETIC
Feel
Touch
Grasp
Hold
Grip
Contact
Solid

AUDITORY DIGITAL
Know
Amend
Make sense
Change
Understand
Notice
Perceive

Sensory preference

Here is a brief generalisation of how to recognise someone's sensory preference and present information accordingly.

Sense	Information preference and traits
Visual	**Prefer:** seeing pictures, diagrams, charts; like things to look nice. **Traits:** speak fast; use visual words; eyes tend to look up when thinking; well-groomed; visual-based job and interests.
Auditory	**Prefer:** discussions and debates,like things to sound right. **Traits:** speak melodically and medium to fast speed; use auditory words; eyes tend to look sideways when thinking; easily distracted by noise; auditory-based job and interests.

Sense	Information preference and traits
Kinaesthetic	**Prefer:** experiencing your ideas; like things to feel right. **Traits:** speak slowly; use kinaesthetic words; eyes tend to look downwards and to the left as you look at them when thinking; tactile/emotional/movement-based job and interests.
Auditory digital	**Prefer:** understanding the facts and rationale; like things to make sense and be logical. **Traits:** use words that are not sensory-specific; eyes tend to look downwards and to the right as you look at them when thinking; analytical job and interests.

How this can work in practice

One of my colleagues speaks openly about her time as a sales representative. She used her knowledge of this topic to improve her sales significantly.

- **For primarily visual clients:** she sent a glossy brochure, and ensured that everything she presented (including her own appearance) looked very neat.

- **For primarily auditory clients:** she talked to them and discussed ideas.

- **For primarily kinaesthetic clients:** where appropriate she let them try out her company's products, or in some way walked them through her proposal.

- **For primarily auditory digital clients:** she gave them the necessary facts and figures.

- **When presenting to a mixed group:** in order to communicate effectively with everyone, she used all four approaches: showing diagrams/charts (visual), having discussions (auditory), providing facts and figures (auditory digital), and giving the audience a chance to participate and experience using her products (kinaesthetic).

Exercise 8.1
Preferred rep system
(1 minute per person)

Tick which you believe is the preferred rep system for important people in your life and/or work (including you!). Remember the following points.

- Some people are equally comfortable with all four main rep systems.

- It is only your guess about someone's preference, not a permanent label.

- Even if someone has a clear preference, it does not mean they cannot or do not use the other systems.

- It may take you a while to collect enough information to fill this in, so do come back to this exercise.

Name	V	A	K	AD

What action will you take as a result of doing Exercise 8.1? For example, if your boss's preferred rep system is auditory, you might want to ensure that you have time to discuss your ideas with him or her face to face and to use more auditory predicates rather than only diagrams or email.

Summary

- Most people have a preference for one or two rep systems.

- If you can use someone's preferred rep system, it will help you communicate with them more effectively as they will be more receptive to your message.

- Practise using predicates when speaking and writing. Listen to people's predicates. Use examples of all four types when communicating with groups (emails, letters, presentations, meetings). Did you notice that the first 14 words of this chapter (including the title) contain four predicates?

Part 3
Using NLP techniques to achieve your goals

Part 3 contains some key NLP techniques that you can use to address typical challenges you may face when striving for your goal, thus increasing the likelihood of your success. Please ensure that where the exercises in this part relate to you making changes, they are ecological (p.4), you are absolutely sure you want to make the changes, and that there are no negative consequences of doing so. Also, the techniques are to be used for minor challenges, not where there are strong negative emotions such as rage, phobias, panic attacks and serious conflicts.

9 Using your inner resources

Imagine being able to choose the state you want to be in (eg calm, energised or confident), and to have these positive emotions at your fingertips in important situations such as interviews and challenging meetings. This chapter will teach you how to do this using a process called 'anchoring'.

Exercise 9.1
When to use anchoring
(2 minutes)

The table below shows some situations when you might want to be able to choose how you feel. Add any other relevant situations.

Interviews	Sporting competitions
Difficult meetings	Negotiations
Appraisals	
Meeting new customers/clients	
Selling	
Exams	
Asking someone out on a date	
Presentations	

Useful states

Depending on the situation, and your own nature, there may be several states that you would like to have access to at your fingertips. The following exercise forms the basis for important exercises later in this chapter.

Exercise 9.2
Useful states

(2 minutes)

Over the page are some states that you might find useful. List situations when you experienced the states.

Confident: ....

....

Motivated: ....

....

Powerful: ....

....

Enthusiastic: ....

....

Strong: ....

....

Energised: ....

....

Focused: ....

....

Calm: ....

....

Relaxed: ....

....

Now list some additional useful states and the situations in which you experienced them.

....

....

....

....

....

....

Anchoring yourself

Here's an overview of how you can quickly set up your own 'anchor' (also known as 'resource anchor') to use when you need to. Let's use confidence as the desired state.

If I asked you to remember a time when you felt *really* confident and relive that experience; see what you're seeing in this situation, hear what you're hearing and really feel the confidence, and then we graphed the intensity of your feelings, it would look something like this ...

Intensity

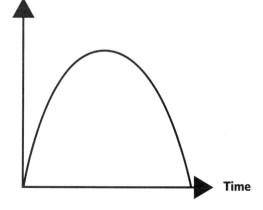

Time

NB: When doing anchoring, it is essential to relive the experience in your mind, so that you can fully feel it, rather than merely thinking about it, which may not evoke the strong feelings.

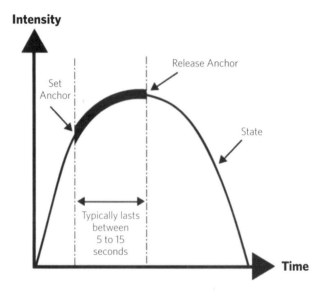

By linking the peak of the intense experience (the thick part of the 'state' line) with a unique and replicable movement (such as squeezing your thumb and index finger together), and repeating this process several times (typically four to six times*), you will have created a strong resource anchor which you can use whenever you need simply by repeating that movement (because the movement and the state will have been neurologically linked).

*When repeating this, either use the same state in each repetition or, for example, use three complementary states twice.

The pneumonic ITURN will help you remember this. ITURN stands for:

- **Intensity** of the experience
- **Timing** of the anchor – capturing the peak of the experience. This generally lasts for 5–15 seconds
- **Uniqueness** of the anchor
- **Replicability** of the anchor
- **Number** of times you repeat it.

Exercise 9.3 will help you to create your own resource anchor.

Exercise 9.3

Feeling at your best

(2 minutes)

1. Think of situations where you would like to feel at your best (from Exercise 9.1).

2. Identify some states that you would like to access in those situations and times when you experienced each individual state (refer to Exercise 9.2).

Future situation: ....

Useful states: ....

....

....

Events when I experienced these states: ....

....

....

....

....

Future situation: ....

Useful states: ....

....

....

Events when I experienced these states: ....

....

....

....

....

Future situation: ....

Useful states: ....

....

....

Events when I experienced these states: ....

....

....

....

....

How to anchor yourself

Read through Exercise 9.4 and the section 'Anchoring yourself' (p.119) enough times so that you know what to do automatically, without having to refer to the book.

Exercise 9.4
Anchoring yourself
(5–10 minutes)

Choose a situation where you would like to feel at your best (refer to Exercise 9.3).

1. Choose the unique and replicable movement you will use to create the anchor. Examples include squeezing your thumb and index finger, or pressing one of your knuckles. Choose the desired state or states you would like to anchor.

2. Pick one desired state and recall a specific time when you felt it. (If by some chance you have not actually experienced it, imagine or pretend that you have.)

3. Relive that (intense) experience – see it, hear it and really feel it.

4. At the peak of the experience, apply the anchor (eg squeeze your thumb and index finger together). Once the peak of the intensity has passed, release the anchor (eg by separating your thumb and index finger).

5. Change your mindset to get out of that particular state ('break state'). You can do this by, for example, thinking of something unrelated, shaking your hands about or walking round the room.

6. Repeat steps 2 to 5, so that you have done this approximately six times. If you have selected three states (as per point 1 in Exercise 9.3), do each of them twice.

7. Test that this has worked by 'firing' the anchor (eg squeezing your thumb and finger together) and noticing how you feel. (If by some chance it has not worked, check that you were really reliving an intense experience as opposed to merely thinking about it.)

Using your anchor

Here are two ways to use the anchor you've set up.

1. Mentally rehearse the event where you would like to feel at your best by:

    a) firing your anchor (ie doing your anchor movement) and seeing yourself as if on a television or cinema screen in several different scenarios, seeing yourself in that really positive state, responding appropriately and well to the different scenarios (eg different questions from interviewers);

    b) as in a), except for seeing, hearing and feeling these scenarios as if they were happening right now.

Notice how much better you now feel about the situation.

2. Before or during the actual situation (for example an interview), if by some chance you feel nervous, fire your anchor so that you feel positive.

In addition, you can top up your resource anchor by repeating steps 2 to 5 in Exercise 9.4 once or twice a day for a month, and also every time something great happens.

Summary

- Your state impacts how you respond.

- You can create your own resource anchor to re-experience ideal states, then use this before or during important or challenging situations (especially those related to your goals) so that you can feel and perform at your best.

10 Seeing other perspectives

Have you ever wished that someone could see things from your point of view? Likewise, *they* probably wish that you could see *their* point of view. In all walks of life, being able to put yourself in the shoes of the other people involved, and to mentally step outside the situation, is an extremely useful skill, because you can then adjust your approach to give you more chance of a successful interaction.

When to use this approach

Exercise 10.1
Situations to see other perspectives
(2 minutes)

The table opposite lists situations when it could be useful to be able to see other perspectives (known in NLP as the 'perceptual positions' technique). Add other situations relevant to you.

Interviews	Coaching
Meetings (general)	
Appraisals	
Selling	
Meeting customers/clients	
Meeting suppliers	
Presentations	
Problem solving	
Planning strategy or projects	
Making decisions	
Writing reports	
Preventing disagreements	
Negotiations	

Some key principles

The perceptual positions technique is based on there being three positions, namely:

- position 1: you
- position 2: the other person(s) involved
- position 3: a neutral observer, or 'wise sage'. Many people can see situations clearly when they are not involved with the situation.

How it works

For the purposes of the explanation, let's assume that you have a job interview with John, and that you would like to have an insight into what he might ask. The process relies on you being willing to 'put yourself in someone else's shoes' (even if you have never met them) and to step back for a few moments. When in position 2 or 3, it is essential to dissociate from yourself and refer to yourself by 'your name' rather than 'me' or 'I'. The diagram on p.137 summarises the technique.

1. Mark out three spaces in the room, ideally equidistant, representing the three perceptual positions (you, John and the neutral observer).

2. Step into position 1, looking towards John's position and notice how you are thinking and feeling; stay there for probably no more than half a minute, so that you are fully experiencing the situation.

3. Move from there and 'break state' (denoted by the lines cutting across the arrows in the diagram on p.137). This is similar to breaking state when anchoring – see point 5 in Exercise 9.4 (p.128).

4. Then step into position 2, as John, and stand or sit as you imagine John would. Look towards 'your name' in position 1. Ask yourself (as John), 'What am I thinking, what am I feeling, what do I want and not want from my meeting with the candidate over there?' It is essential that you take on John's persona, and answer as if you were him or imagine him to be. For example, 'What I want from the candidate is ....' or even 'What I want from you is ...'. Position 2 is where the insights normally start. Keep asking yourself (as John) these questions until there are no more useful answers.

5. Move from position 2 and break state.

6. Step into position 3 as a neutral observer, seeing 'the interviewer and the interviewee' (not 'him' and 'me') over there. Ask yourself, as the wise observer, questions such as:

   ■ 'What do I notice about those two people (ie John and "your name")?'

   ■ 'What do they both want?'

   ■ 'What advice would I give "your name"?', and 'How would John respond if "your name" did that?'

7. Then take the learnings and insights back to position 1, as yourself, and decide on a course of action. If you would like, re-visit position 2 and/or 3. Please make sure you return to posistion 1 to complete the exercise.

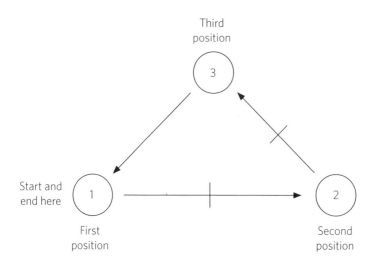

Breaking state

When doing the perceptual positions technique, it is essential to break state in order to be out of your own mindset and, as far as possible, in the mindset of the people in positions 2 and 3. Most people find it easy to know how they see and feel about the situation. The learnings come from putting yourself in someone else's shoes.

Exercise 10.2
Perceptual positions
(10 minutes per situation)

Pick a situation (perhaps related to one of your goals from
Chapter 3) where you would benefit from seeing another
perspective. Do the perceptual positions exercise on the previous
pages and note the key learnings and action points on pp.139–140.

Situation A: ....

Key learnings and action points

Situation B: ....

Key learnings and action points

Summary

■ There is always more than one way to look at a situation.

■ Being willing to consider how other people could perceive a situation, or how you would advise others in the situation, will help you in the examples mentioned in Exercise 10.1.

■ When doing perceptual positions, it is important that you really put yourself in the mindset of the relevant people.

■ You may wish to revisit Exercise 6.1 (p.77) with your new knowledge.

11 Staying positive

The Communication Model (Chapter 6) explains how our perception of events impacts on our experience. Some people see a glass as half empty, others as half full. Being able to see the positives in situations is one of the keys to a happy life. 'Reframing' is the process of putting a positive spin on events, which will help you to be resilient if there are minor setbacks or challenges on the path to your goals.

When is reframing useful?

Reframing is useful for relatively minor events, not catastrophes. Examples of situations for reframing include the following.

- Feeling negative because your boss keeps asking you questions about your work.

- Not being successful at an interview.

- Someone refusing to go on a date with you.

- Your teenage child being too headstrong.

How to reframe yourself

If you find yourself in a situation where you are a little upset about something (such as a temporary setback regarding your goal), step back and ask yourself questions such as the following.

- 'Where or when else would this other person's behaviour be useful?'

- 'What else could this behaviour/situation mean?'

- 'What have I not seen/noticed about this situation which would put a different spin on it?'

- 'How would a really positive person view this?'

- 'How could I look on the bright side?'

Not all of these questions will be relevant in each circumstance. A reframe is just another possible, plausible and more positive way of looking at a situation rather than a 'negative' way you may otherwise have. It is not about advising yourself what action to take. Often, lightening up and laughing are useful and help you reframe.

Using the examples just given, here are some possible reframes.

Situation: Feeling negative because my boss keeps asking me questions about my work.

Possible reframe(s):

1. Perhaps she's just showing interest.

2. Perhaps she wants to learn from me.

3. At least this boss shows some interest. The last one didn't!

Situation: Not being successful at an interview.

Possible reframe(s):

1. At least I learned some things for my next interview.

2. It probably wasn't the right job for me anyway.

3. There'll be something better round the corner.

4. I've overcome disappointments before and gone on to better things.

Situation: Someone refusing to go on a date with you.

Possible reframe(s):

1. That's his loss.

2. At least I can now look for someone who is right for me.

3. Glad I didn't waste much time on him

Situation: My teenager is too headstrong – he's always arguing with me.

Possible reframe(s):

1. Isn't it great that he'll be able to stand up for himself when he starts his career?

2. Thankfully he's going to university next year.

3. I'd be more concerned if he didn't argue with me.

Exercise 11.1
Reframing yourself
(1 minute per situation)

Pick a minor challenge or disappointment that you have experienced or are experiencing. What are the positives about this situation?

Situation: ....

Possible reframe(s): ....

....

....

....

Situation: ....

Possible reframe(s): ....

....

....

....

Situation: ....

Possible reframe(s): ....

....

....

....

Situation: ....

Possible reframe(s): ....

....

....

....

If you find yourself feeling negative about something in the future, take a moment to reframe and find the positives.

Summary

■ You can choose whether to see the positives or the negatives in any situation.

■ Reframing will help you stay positive if there are hiccups along the route to you achieving your goal(s).

■ The more positive your attitude the more resilient and successful you'll be.

12

Changing beliefs

As we discussed in Chapter 6, beliefs are our current thinking about a topic. They can be either useful or limiting, and are an important factor determining our results. This chapter looks at how you can remove some limiting beliefs that get in the way of you achieving your goals.

Most people at some time in their life experience limiting beliefs about:

- themselves or their capabilities (eg 'I can't learn to swim well')
- other people (eg 'my boss is a really miserable person')
- the way the world works (eg 'salespeople aren't trustworthy').

In this chapter we'll look at some ways to reduce or even remove such relatively minor beliefs.

Exercise 12.1
Limiting beliefs
(2 minutes)

Over the page list any minor limiting beliefs you have become aware of during this book. Minor limiting beliefs tend to relate to the three categories in the bullet points on the opposite page, and whilst they may cause the person who has the belief to feel a little upset, they generally will not lead to a strong negative emotion like anger, rage or despair. In addition to the examples given in brackets, other examples of minor limiting beliefs could be the following.

- 'I can't learn to play the violin.'

- 'I'll never be able to do good presentations.'

- 'I'll never be able to do well at interviews.'

My limiting beliefs

Belief busting

Here are some ways for you to change any minor limiting beliefs, either by completely removing them, or at least reducing the extent to which you believe in them. Not all of these will be relevant in every situation.

- **Look for counter-examples.** Ask yourself, 'where or when has this belief not been true either for me or other people?' One of my clients (a management consultant) believed she couldn't sell to big companies, until I challenged her and she was then able to name some of the many big companies she had sold to!

- **Use perceptual positions** (Chapter 10). Often, putting yourself in someone else's shoes, or imagining a situation as a neutral observer, will change how you perceive the situation.

- **Use reframing** (Chapter 11). Look for the positive elements of the situation.

- **Check your reality.** Sometimes we make assumptions and then start believing them. It could be worth asking yourself, 'How do I know this belief is true?', or even 'How do I know this belief isn't false?'

- **Increase your capabilities.** Limiting beliefs may result from lack of skills. Using the example of the management consultant on p.157, even if she were unable to sell to big companies, learning additional sales skills would have helped her.

- **Pretend.** Ask yourself, 'What would someone who could do this do? How would they act?', and then do that. 'Fake it until you make it!'

- **Use the mindset for success.** Revisit the positive beliefs covered in Chapter 5. Behave as if these are true. Remember to be 'at cause'.

- **Use your resource anchor.** One of my clients was due to present to a big conference the following day. She was nervous, and believed that the audience would not be receptive to her. She used her resource anchor (see Chapter 9) and the presentation went so well that a journalist in the audience asked to interview her.

- **What's your purpose?** Refer to some of the goal-setting questions (Chapter 3, pp.28 and 29). Sometimes getting in touch with your values, sense of purpose will help you find the motivation to overcome a limiting belief.

- **You've changed beliefs before.** Almost all of us have believed we couldn't do something, and yet found later that we could. Think now of at least five times when you have done this (eg run a 10km race, been promoted). Could the current limiting belief simply be another example of a belief which has reached its sell-by date, or soon will?

Summary

- Your beliefs are merely your current thinking about a topic.

- If you have any beliefs that limit you, there are numerous ways to minimise or negate their impact.

Conclusion: moving forward

By reading this book and doing the exercises, you already have knowledge that will take you towards achieving not only the goals you set in **Part 1**, but also those you will set in the future.

Part 2 provided you with some of the fundamental communication skills within NLP that will help you in all your endeavours, certainly in achieving your goals.

Part 3 added some specific NLP techniques to give you the edge over people who do not have this knowledge.

I recommend that you:

- revisit this book and its exercises regularly to keep the material fresh in your mind
- reassess your Wheel of Life, values and goals every year, to ensure that you are being at cause and taking your life in the direction *you* want
- Be 100% at cause.

Learning more about NLP

You may find that the knowledge and benefits that you have gained from this introductory NLP book has sparked your curiosity to see how much more you could achieve. If so, there are several ways to extend your knowledge.

- Take a look at another of my books, *Successful NLP* (Crimson, 2010), which provides more comprehensive information about NLP techniques. There are numerous audio and video materials available both physically and electronically.

- If you are interested, look into training courses. There are numerous entry-level courses available, ranging from brief introduction workshops through to a four-day Diploma and a 125-hour NLP Practitioner course.

- My website, www.thelazarus.com, contains information about our training courses and our books, audio and video material. It also contains a free guide to what to consider when choosing an NLP course.

Thank you for allowing me to be your teacher and guide in this introduction to achieving your goals with NLP. I wish you every success in your life.

Further reading and useful resources

Books

NLP modelling

- Dilts, Robert, *Modelling with NLP* (Meta Publications, 1998)

NLP general

- Bodenhamer, Bob and Hall, L Michael, *The User's Manual For The Brain Volume I and Volume II* (Crown House Publishing, 1999 and 2003 respectively).

- Lazarus, Jeremy, *Successful NLP: For The Results You Want* (Crimson Publishing, 2010)

- O'Connor, Joseph, *NLP Workbook: A practical guide to achieving the results you want* (Element (HarperCollins), 2001)

- Wake, Lisa, *NLP: Principles in Practice* (Ecademy Press, 2010)

NLP coaching

- O'Connor, Joseph and Lages, Andrea, *Coaching with NLP: A practical guide to getting the best out of yourself and others* (Element (HarperCollins), 2004).

NLP reference and encyclopaedia

- Dilts, Robert and DeLozier, Judith, *Encyclopaedia of Systemic Neuro-Linguistic Programming and NLP New Coding* (NLP University Press, 2000)

NLP health

- Dilts, Robert, Hallbom, Tim and Smith, Suzi, *Beliefs – Pathways to Health & Well-Being* (Metamorphous Press, 1990)

NLP selling

- Johnson, Kerry L, *Selling with NLP* (Nicholas Brealey Publishing, 1994)

- O'Connor, Joseph and Prior, Robin, *Successful Selling With NLP: Powerful ways to help you connect with your customers* (Thorsons (HarperCollins), 1995)

NLP sport

- Lazarus, Jeremy, *Ahead of the Game: How to Use Your Mind to Win in Sport* (Ecademy Press, 2006)

- There are various e-books on the mental aspects of sport (based on NLP techniques) available on www.winningatsport.com, a website owned by the author dedicated to the uses of NLP in sport

NLP work

- Knight, Sue, *NLP At Work: The Difference That Makes the Difference* (Nicholas Brealey Publishing, 1995)

Also available from the author

- *The NLP Pocket Handbook.* An 80-page, A6 guide to the NLP Practitioner and Master Practitioner material. Available from www.thelazarus.com

Audio material

There are several providers of NLP-related audio material ranging from one or two topics through to Practitioner and Master Practitioner level CD sets.

Also available from the author

The following CDs are available from The Lazarus Consultancy, covering most of the topics contained in this book.

- *NLP Practitioner CD Series.* A 16-CD set, lasting approximately 12.5 hours, with a fully-referenced training manual. This comprises the pre-study material for The Lazarus Consultancy Fast-Track NLP Practitioner Course

- *Understanding, Predicting and Influencing Behaviour – 4 CD Series.* Lasting 4.5 hours, this covers Values and Meta Programmes (personality traits) with a fully-referenced manual

- *Understanding, Predicting and Influencing Behaviour – 6 CD NLP Series.* Lasting 6 hours, this covers Values and Meta Programmes plus a fully-referenced manual. In addition, the CDs cover how to change Values and Deep Filters, and for that reason are of relevance mainly to NLP Practitioners and Master Practitioners

Other audio material

The author will be developing further audio and DVD material, including interviews. These will be available on both www.thelazarus.com and www.winningatsport.com.

Websites

- www.anlp.org. The Association of NLP International (UK-based)

- http://nlpuniversitypress.com. This is the web version of the Encyclopaedia of Systemic Neuro-Linguistic Programming and NLP New Coding